LAKE TAHOE

A Picture Book to Remember Her by

CRESCENT BOOKS
NEW YORK

CLB 1700
© 1987 Colour Library Books Ltd, Godalming, Surrey, England.
All rights reserved.
This 1991 edition published by Crescent Books,
distributed by Outlet Book Company, Inc, a Random House Company,
225 Park Avenue South, New York, New York 10003.
Printed in Hong Kong.
ISBN 0 517 62360 9
8 7 6 5 4 3 2

Acknowledgement
The publishers gratefully acknowledge the loan of illustrations and the kind
assistance provided by Lake Tahoe Visitors Authority (photographs pages
20, 21, 28 bottom, 29). Heavenly Valley Resort (photographs pages 22-27
and 28 top), and Caesars Tahoe (photographs page 10).

There are dozens of lakes in the world bigger than Tahoe, four or five are even deeper. But with a shoreline of 71 miles, Lake Tahoe is big enough to impress anybody. Its surface area is 193 square miles, which should make it something of a landmark to anyone who ventures near it. But until 1860, hardly anybody knew it was there.

To be sure, there are plenty of landmarks in the American West that no one noticed until the last half of the 19th century, but thousands passed within a dozen miles of this one during the great California gold rush that began in 1849, and hundreds more had glimpses of it as they went over mountain passes into California long before that.

Even the mountain men and trappers who got to know the Sierra Nevada Mountains like the backs of their hands in the early part of the century were only vaguely aware that there was a big lake up there at 6,228 feet. The forces that created it boxed it in so that it can't be seen from the Truckee Pass a few miles away, and while the Carson Pass below the lake allows a few glimpses of sparkling blue, figuring out how to get up there was a problem.

In the early 1850s some westward-bound emigrants tried to use the lake as a shortcut, but most found disaster for their trouble. Possible disaster and a little trouble didn't matter a bit after the spring of 1859, when some prospectors hunting for gold discovered that the black gravel they had been discarding was really silver and it was worth nearly $850 a ton. That summer, men who had headed west over the mountains a few years before began rushing back to the east side. The Tahoe Valley provided a shorter route, even if it was more hazardous, and time was of the essence.

By the end of the summer there was almost as much traffic past Lake Tahoe as there is today. And not all of it was passing through. In no time there were hotels and general stores, and by the following spring there were two sawmills working around the clock to meet the needs of the mining camps around the famous Comstock Lode on the Nevada side.

The road was improved in 1863. It was watered to keep the dust down in summer and plowed clear of snow in winter, and for the next five years there was a steady stream of traffic in both directions. By 1880, the glory days of Virginia City and the camps in the Comstock area were over. But the glory never left Lake Tahoe, whose settlers had made more than the miners a little further east. There were more than a dozen dairies that couldn't produce butter fast enough to sell at 42 cents a pound. The price of Tahoe-produced hay for the Comstock livestock never dropped below $25 a ton. And trout from the lake were bringing 25 cents a pound. Charges for freight brought them another $12 million a year, and much of the freight heading east was lumber, or the produce of local farms.

When it was all over and the prospectors moved on, there was never a thought that any of the towns on the shores of Lake Tahoe would go the way of Virginia City and become ghost towns. Stagecoach companies began scheduling tours to see the lake's natural wonders and local residents were ready for them. As early as 1876 one of the local sawmills was converted into a luxury hotel. The new millionaires from Virginia City chose it as the site of elegant homes away from home. Fancy excursion boats came next, carrying tourists from one expensive hotel to another or just carrying them out on the lake for the sheer pleasure of a boat ride.

In the 1890s a narrow-gauge railroad brought visitors up the Truckee Canyon from the main line of the Southern Pacific. The destination was the Tahoe Tavern, one of the most famous hotels in the world in its heyday. It was also one of the most expensive. But the experience of visiting this place so removed from the rest of the world seemed worth any price.

Everything was, and still is, perfect for getting away from it all. The climate, in summer at least, is delightful. There are no pesky insects, no poisonous snakes, and every now and then there is a summer snow shower to give visitors something to write about on the backs of their postcards. There is beautiful back country to explore and beautiful scenery right out the front door.

They stayed away in winter in the '90s, but today some people think that's the best time to go to Lake Tahoe, where there are more than a half dozen ski resorts within a dozen miles of Tahoe City. In summer, there is boating and camping and swimming and there are still plenty of fish left. There is gambling on the Nevada side and for those who prefer gamboling across meadows covered with wild flowers or through thick, evergreen forests, there is no place on earth quite like it. Think what all those people missed when they wandered past and didn't even know it was there.

Dep. Leg. B-36490-87

Facing page: sailing craft on the shore at South Lake Tahoe.

South Lake Tahoe and Stateline (these and previous pages), are the busiest, most visited of the lake's resorts, the former offering horseback-riding, fishing, camping, golf, tennis, hiking and a variety of water sports among its summer pursuits. Stateline, just over the border into Nevada, offers the chief accommodation at the south end of the lake. Being the only place in America outside of Atlantic City where casino gambling is legal, Nevada attracts many visitors all year round. Lake Tahoe's water (facing page bottom) is as clear as glass; in 1872 Mark Twain observed in his "Roughing It" that "where it was only twenty or thirty feet deep the bottom was so perfectly distinct that the boat seemed floating in the air!" Ringed by the Sierra Nevada (below) to the east and the Carson Range to the west, Lake Tahoe's surface elevation is 6,229 feet above sea level and, measuring 12 by 22 miles, it is the largest alpine lake in North America.

The lake hosts a wide range of exciting water sports (previous pages and facing page bottom). Caesar's Tahoe (this page), one of many casinos just over the border in Nevada, offers all manner of gaming facilities. Facing page top: Eldorado County Beach, South Lake Tahoe.

Above: a view from Heavenly Valley of one of Lake Tahoe's matchless sunsets. Highway 50 (left), the old overland route which brought settlers to California, affords glorious views of forest slopes and river canyons as it winds its way from Sacramento to the south end of the lake. Facing page: sporting activities on and around Lake Tahoe cater for every taste, from yachting to horse-riding. Overleaf: Eldorado County Beach (left), just south of the border, offers numerous overnight camp-sites, picnic areas and a jetty in idyllic surroundings. (Right top) a water skiier takes advantage of the lake's early-morning calm. The *Tahoe Queen* (right bottom), an authentic paddlewheeler with a glass bottom, cruises across Lake Tahoe year round. Trips vary from the daily cruises to Emerald Bay – taking in the sights of Vikingsholm Castle and Cave Rock – to Ski-Shuttle runs in the winter and spring.

The Tahoe Keys Marina (these pages and overleaf), South Lake Tahoe, is populated with pleasure craft of every shape and size imaginable. There is plenty of room for sail, motor and paddle boats on the lake's 193 square acres of water, however. Fishing on the lake is good for Mackinaw, silver, brown, cutthroat, rainbow and eastern brook trout. Kokanee salmon, introduced to the lake in 1940, may also be caught in selected waters. Licences valid for fishing anywhere on the lake may be bought in either state. The shoreline buildings on Tahoe Keys Marina, constructed chiefly from natural materials, blend pleasantly with their surroundings, retaining the charm, if not quite the appearance, of the old log cabins which they have replaced. The mountains of the Toiyabe National Forest, one of the three which surround the lake, provide a stunning backdrop to this, the lake's south end.

On average, the Sierra Nevada receives 20 feet of fine powdery snow each winter. As a result there are in excess of 20 ski areas in the Lake Tahoe Basin alone. Although known primarily for its intensive development and compactness, the region also boasts America's most expansive ski resort, Heavenly Valley (overleaf), covering a remarkable 20 square miles of High Sierra peaks. Each resort provides ski rental and instruction and most have a variety of slopes and lifts, while the breathtaking scenery (above) is shared by all. The character of each resort depends very much on its situation. Heavenly Valley for instance, being located at South Lake Tahoe, is popular with those who come not only for the sport but also for the gambling, while Northstar, on the opposite side of the lake, caters mainly to families. The snow on the downhill slopes in the late evening (facing page) offers speed and excitement.

STANDINGS

Heavenly Valley resort (these pages and overleaf), with lodges on both sides of the border, offers clearly-marked runs for skiers of all abilities. Top: the slopes of Heavenly Valley run smoothly down towards the beautiful blue lake. The resort's aerial tram (facing page) lifts sightseers and skiers alike 2,000 feet above the lake to experience what Mark Twain once called "the fairest view the whole earth affords."

All sorts of skiing: (top right) cross country and (top) formation, popular at Kirkwood (facing page bottom), and (above) competitive and (facing page top) helicopter skiing, providing excitement at Heavenly. Right: free-style fun on the slopes.

The viewpoint (these and previous pages) at the summit of Heavenly Valley's aerial tram is constantly visited and never forgotten. The lake's full 72 miles of shoreline, surrounded by the majestic, snow-topped mountains of the Sierra Nevada and the Carson Range, may be seen from this spot. Open all year round, the tram runs for a mile, climbing to an elevation of 8,250 feet, where a popular restaurant and an outdoor café (facing page) command beautiful panoramic views. The virtually cloudless alpine sky constantly changes hue throughout the day, is reflected in the deep waters of the lake lends infinite variations in mood to the scene,. Below: the subtle tones and colors of sky and lake contrast dramatically with the blackness of the mountains. Overleaf: the brilliant blue waters and golden sand of Pope Beach at the southern end of the lake, with Fallen Leaf Lake and the Sierra Nevada mountains in the background.

Mount Tallac (these pages and overleaf) on the southwest shore, distinguished by its snow cross, is one of the jewels in the crown of the Sierra Nevada, the highest unified mountain range in America. Just over the front ridge of the range, beyond Mount Tallac, lies the Desolation Wilderness area, frequented by those who wish, quite literally, to "get away from it all." This 63,475-acre, roadless expanse boasts peaks, canyons, mountain basins, tumbling streams and no less than 70 named lakes. Fishing, boating, back-packing, camping and horseback riding are all here to be enjoyed by those who prefer the peace of Lake Tahoe's alpine countryside to its hustle and bustle in Stateline. Left and facing page top: children enjoy one of the east shore's sandy beaches and (top) pleasure craft dot the lake's deep blue waters. Though normally calm, summer thunderstorms can cause these waters to become rough and inhospitable. The ponderosa pine (facing page top and overleaf) dominates Lake Tahoe's vegetation and cloaks the valley slopes in green.

These pages and overleaf: Emerald Bay, the most picturesque spot on the lake. The pristine waters of this inlet encompass the lake's only island and are visited by cruisers (above) daily. Facing page bottom: pastel perfection bathes the scene at sunrise.

These pages and overleaf: due to unusual atmospheric conditions in the area, some remarkable light effects are achieved on the lake's surface, its colors running the gamut of the entire spectrum. Blues range from deepest sapphire to palest powder in the cool stillness of early morning (above). Emerald Bay (remaining pictures), so called because of its splendid green color (right), assumes many and varied guises. Facing page: soft, honey-colored rays envelop the well-known beauty spot late on a summer's evening, blurring the horizon and casting golden highlights on the bows of moored sailing boats. Overleaf: sunset cloaks the bay with a rich fiery coloring, silhouetting the ponderosa pines and Fannette Island.

Eagle Falls (above and facing page bottom), a short walk from Emerald Bay (facing page top), afford spectacular panoramic views. Right: a view from the weaving Highway 89, on the approach to the lake. Top: pine trees cling to the steep, rocky slopes behind Emerald Bay. Overleaf: Cascade Lake.

This page: D. L. Bliss State Park, on the west shore. This large, mountainous park offers forestland and long stretches of sandy beach. Swimming, boating and picnicking are all excellent here, and the comprehensive camping facilities attract many visitors in the summer season. Some extraordinary effects on the color of the lake are brought about by the varying depth of the water. The stepping of the lake's bed off the west shore (facing page top) may be distinctly reproduced in the surface coloration. Facing page bottom: the boat launch at picturesque Meeks Bay. This west-shore spot also offers a camping ground and boasts spectacular easterly views across the lake to the jagged outline of the Sierra Nevada. Overleaf: Emerald Bay, said to be the most photographed scene in the United States. The bay is entirely within D. L. Bliss and Emerald Bay state parks.

There are all manner of water activities to be enjoyed on and around Lake Tahoe. Meeks Bay (above and top) is a popular point at which to "take the plunge" and the Truckee River (left and facing page top) offers exciting rafting. Facing page bottom: the Olympic Valley Inn.

Truckee (below, right and bottom), once a busy railroad town, still retains much of the character of the Old West. Bottom right: The Spur casino in Carson City, Nevada's State Capital. Facing page: Virginia City, a well-preserved frontier mining town, typical of the late 19th century, about 30 miles east of the lake.

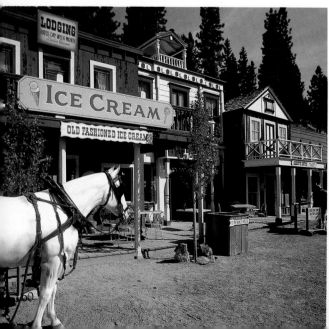

Previous pages: (left) the Ponderosa
Ranch, Incline Village, home of the
television show "Bonanza" and (right) the
sandy north shore. Zephyr Cove (above,
facing page top and overleaf), just north of
Stateline, offers a long beach of golden
sand and facilities for many water sports.
Right: Cave Rock, a distinctive landmark
in a beautiful cove (facing page bottom).